Jim Henson's

RETURN TO LABYRINTH™

Volume 2

Written by Jake T. Forbes
Illustrated by Chris Lie
Cover Art by Kouyu Shurei

Based on the feature film "Labyrinth"
Directed by Jim Henson
Story by Dennis Lee and Jim Henson
Screenplay by Terry Jones

Original designs by Brian Froud

HAMBURG // LONDON // LOS ANGELES // TOKYO

Jim Henson's Return to Labyrinth Vol. 2
Written by Jake T. Forbes
Illustrated by Chris Lie

Inkers - Dyotami Febriani and Rhoald Marcellius of
Imaginary Friends Studios
Tones - Infinity Studio
Lettering - Lucas Rivera
Cover Design - Anne Marie Horne & Kouyu Shurei

Consulting Editor - Michael Polis
Assistant Editor - Sarah Tangney

Editor - Tim Beedle
Digital Imaging Manager - Chris Buford
Pre-Production Supervisor - Erika Terriquez
Managing Editor - Elisabeth Brizzi
Creative Director - Anne Marie Horne
Editor-in-Chief - Rob Tokar
Publisher - Mike Kiley
President and C.O.O. - John Parker
C.E.O. and Chief Creative Officer - Stuart Levy

A  Manga

TOKYOPOP Inc.
5900 Wilshire Blvd. Suite 2000
Los Angeles, CA 90036

E-mail: info@TOKYOPOP.com
Come visit us online at www.TOKYOPOP.com

© 1986, 2007 The Jim Henson Company. All rights reserved. No portion of this book may be
LABYRINTH is a trademark of The Jim Henson Company. reproduced or transmitted in any form or by any means
Labyrinth characters © 1986 Labyrinth Enterprises. without written permission from the copyright holders.
All Rights Reserved. This manga is a work of fiction. Any resemblance to
actual events or locales or persons, living or dead, is
entirely coincidental.

ISBN: 978-1-59816-726-9

First TOKYOPOP printing: October 2007
10 9 8 7 6 5 4 3 2 1
Printed in the USA

Contents

Previously...

Toby Williams was just an ordinary boy with ordinary problems: homework, girls and parents.

Or so he thought.

A visit from his mysterious new guidance counselor caps a series of increasingly bizarre encounters and occurrences. First, there was his ruined school play. Then he was mistakenly accused of cheating on his calculus test. Finally, after catching something making off with his history paper, he follows the small creature through a hidden passage in his closet and out into a remarkable new world.

Determined to find the thief, he continues his pursuit, only to be accosted by Hana, a faerie who has lost her wings, and her furry companion, Stank. Upon discovering that they could both work together to achieve their individual goals, Hana decides to team up with Toby. They catch up to the thief, a small goblin named Skub, only to find that he no longer has the history paper and that Toby's homework is, in fact, at the castle that rests at the center of the huge Labyrinth that dominates the kingdom. Promising to help Toby and his friends make their way through the maze, Skub joins their party. Unfortunately, some problems in the Labyrinth land Toby in jail, where he meets Moppet, a girl disguised as a goblin, and Spittledrum, the goblin mayor who orders Toby to be put to death.

However, his execution is unexpectedly halted by someone Toby instantly recognizes: his new guidance counselor. He reveals himself to be Jareth, the Goblin King (who seems to share some sort of history with Toby's sister) and promises to return Toby to his world if Toby agrees to attend Jareth's ball that evening. He does, and Toby finds himself drinking and dining among such individuals as Hoggle, the Prince of the Land of Stench, Sir Didymous, a very chivalrous fox, and Queen Mizumi of the Moraine Kingdom, a coldly beautiful woman who seems to put people on edge.

It's a breathtaking evening and a ball unlike any other, but Toby can't help feeling out of place. Therefore, he certainly wasn't prepared for the evening's big announcement. Jareth has decided to retire and has chosen none other than Toby as the next Goblin King and Lord of the Labyrinth.

Chapter 1
MIZUMI'S PROPOSITION

THE GOBLINS ARE REVOLTING!

REALLY, SPITTLEDRUM, MUST YOU ALWAYS DWELL ON THE OBVIOUS? THEY ARE POSITIVELY VILE.

Chapter 2
KING TOBY

C'MON, STANK. LET'S GET OUT OF THESE SUITS AND FIND TOBY.

NOT SO FAST, VERMIN.

YOU TWO AREN'T OFF THE HOOK YET. GET SCRUBBING.

IT'S OKAY. THEY'RE WITH ME.

SPLSH

ESKER, FETCH OUR BAGS. IT APPEARS WE'LL HAVE TO BIDE OUR TIME UNTIL THE APPOINTED HOUR.

YES, MILADY.

COME ALONG, MY DEARS.

Meanwhile...

I EXPRESSLY ORDERED YOU TO STAY HERE!

HIDEOUS? WHY, IT'S MADE FROM PIECES OF *YOU*, TOBY.

THE SKIN IS MADE FROM FLAKES OF YOUR OWN SKIN. THE HAIR IS YOUR HAIR. EVEN THE TOENAILS HAVE BEEN FASHIONED FROM ACTUAL CLIPPINGS FROM YOUR FEET.

THAT'S *REVOLTING!*

MY DEAR BOY, *THIS* IS REVOLTING.

BUT YOU'VE HAD A TRYING TWO DAYS, AND I CAN UNDERSTAND WHY YOU'D BE CONFUSED.

NO, I BELIEVE THE WORD YOU INTENDED WAS "MAGNIFICENT."

AH, THANK YOU.

OF COURSE, IF WE HAD FRESHER MATERIALS TO WORK WITH, THE LIKENESS WOULD BE *MUCH* MORE ACCURATE.

IT WASN'T EASY, YOU KNOW. YOU HUMANS SHED VERY TINY PIECES. SOMETIMES I WISH YOU WERE A REPTILE. MUCH EASIER TO REPRODUCE.

YOU DON'T ALWAYS GET WHAT YOU WANT.

BUT...
...

...YOU'LL FIND SOME-TIMES THAT YOU GET...

...

WHAT YOU NEED.

I WAS GATHERING MOSS WAITING FOR YOU TO FINISH UP!

WHAT YOU NEED.

Chapter 3
EDUCATING TOBY

WAIT--

AAAARRGHH!!!

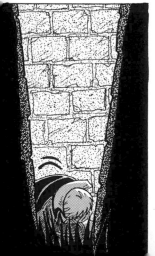

CLICK

THIS IS SO HUMILIATING...

PAT PAT

NOW, WHICH ONE WAS IT AGAIN...?

OH, OF COURSE!

AND TO THINK SHE SOLVED THIS THING ON HER FIRST TRY WITHOUT ANY MAGIC...
Sigh...

LIKE *MAGIC.*

WITCH!

WHAT

POP

DID YOU

POP

DO WITH

POP

MY VOICE?!

POP

I CAN TEACH YOU HOW, AS WELL AS TECHNIQUES MUCH MORE IMPRESSIVE THAN THAT LITTLE TRICK. I SENSE YOU HAVE THE POTENTIAL TO BE EVERY BIT AS POWERFUL A SORCERER AS JARETH.

EVEN MORE SO.

I'M SURE THAT IS WHY HE PICKED *YOU* AS HIS HEIR.

Second Period: Drama

STEP 2--ADD GERMS.

ALLOW ME.

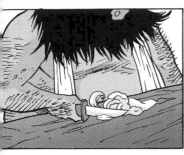

PLOP

STEP 3--WAIT 12 HOURS--

FWP FWP FWP FWP

CURDS, WHEY, RINDS... SKUB CAN NEVER MAKE CHEESE BEFORE DINNER!

sob sob

My wings have got to be around here somewhere.

Chapter 4
SECRET PLACES

THE BOY'S A *DOLT.*

MOTHER?

A DUMMY! A DUNCE! A HALFWIT! A BOOB!

MOTHER!

Don't say boob.

IT'S SO BEAUTIFUL...

WHOEVER SLEPT HERE MUST HAVE BEEN AWFULLY IMPORTANT.

IMPORTANT, HUH? THEN HOW DO YOU EXPLAIN THE DOOR? IT'S LIKE SOMETHING OUT OF A *PRISON*.

IT WAS PROBABLY JUST FOR SECURITY. TO KEEP OUT THIEVING FAERIES.

WHO'S THIEVING?!

HUH...?

CHECK OUT THE FANCY THREADS...

FASHION SHOW! FASHION SHOW!

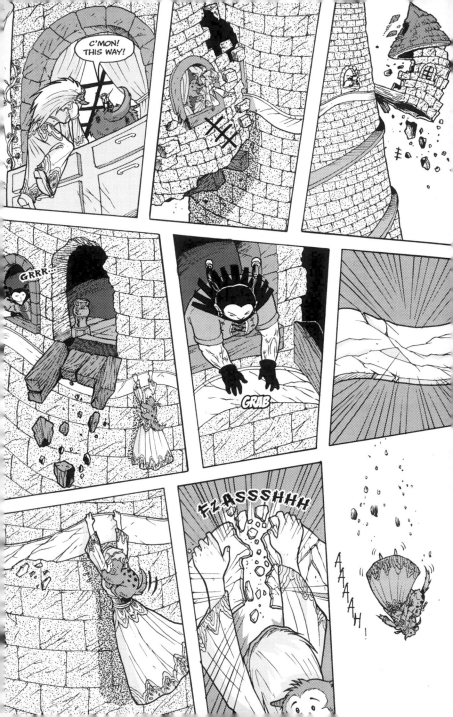

To Be Continued...

Toby has completed his education, but is he truly ready to wear the crown and take control of the Labyrinth?

The answer to that lies with the Pathmaker, and frankly, when it comes to all things Toby, the Pathmaker just ain't talking.

Then there's the matter of those two little lizards. What news do they bring? And just how do they "fit" into our story?

It goes without saying that Mizumi's not going to be happy with Drumlin, but why does Moppet look so much like Sarah?

And let's talk about Toby's sister for a moment... Actually, on second thought, let's not. We have to save something for the next volume, don't we?

DON'T MISS OUR THIRD EXCITING INSTALLMENT!

Guest Art Gallery

Heidi Arnhold

Pop Mhan

Erica Reis

Nichol

Amy Mebberson

Ocala Bellows Kulig

Tim Smith 3

TS3

Through DANGERS untold and hardships UNNUMBERED

I have fought my way here, to the castle beyond the GOBLIN CITY

to take back the CHILD you have STOLEN

For my WILL is as STRONG as yours, and my KINGDOM is as GREAT.

YOU have NO POWER over ME

Tintin Pantoja

Chrissy Delk

- GEORGE ALEXOPOULOS

George Alexopoulos

Jessica Feinberg

Should You Need Us...

Amy Mcbberson

Just fear me

Love me

Do as I say...

...and I will be your slave.

Guest Art Contributors

Heidi Arnhold is a recent graduate from the Savannah College of Art and Design and the illustrator of *Jim Henson's Legends of the Dark Crystal,* available from TOKYOPOP in November 2007. You can find more of her work at http://chibimaryn.deviantart.com.

Pop Mhan has been drawing comics for Marvel, DC and Dark Horse for the past ten years. He is the creator of *Blank,* available now from TOKYOPOP, and has illustrated issues of *Batgirl, Marvel Adventures Spider-Man* and *Robin.* Visit him on the Web at www.popmhan.com.

Erica Reis is also a recent graduate of the Savannah College of Art and Design and is the creator of *Sea Princess Azuri,* the second volume of which is available now from TOKYOPOP. Discover the underwater world of the Orcans (and say hi to Erica) at www.seaprincessazuri.com.

Nichol is a recent winner of TOKYOPOP's *Rising Stars of Manga* contest and a graduate of the Art Institute of Boston. You can find more of her comics work at www.nixcomix.com.

Amy Mebberson is also a winner of the *Rising Stars of Manga* contest and the co-creator of TOKYOPOP's original manga series *Divalicious!*, as well as the popular Web comic *As If!* Her most recent Web comic, *Thorn*, can be found on her Web site: www.mimisgrotto.com.

Ocala Bellows Kulig is an illustrator and video game concept designer. Her most recent projects include *City of Villains* and *Star Trek Online.* Check out more of her art at www.pixelimn.com.

Tim Smith 3 is the creator of the original manga series *Grimm & Co.*, coming soon from TOKYOPOP. He's also worked on *The Hardy Boys* and *Tales from the Crypt* for Papercutz. His Web domain is www.timsmith3.com.

Tintin Pantoja graduated from the School of Visual Arts in New York. She's since illustrated John Wiley & Sons' manga adaptation of *Hamlet* and is currently working on TOKYOPOP's adaptation of *Pride & Prejudice.* See pages from both at http://mentacle.rusticeye.com.

Chrissy Delk is also a recent graduate from the Savannah College of Art and Design. She's the co-creator of *Paintings of You*, available now from Iris Print, and *Wonderland*, a fantasy Web comic that you can read at *www.amadteaparty.net.*

George Alexopoulos is a winner of the *Rising Stars of Manga* contest and the creator of *Go With Grace*, a single-volume graphic novel available from TOKYOPOP. You can see more of his comics work at *www.studionj.com.*

Jessica Feinberg is a freelance illustrator and the toner of *Jim Henson's Legends of the Dark Crystal*. She's also the English-language localizer for such manga series as *Mitsukazu Mihara: The Embalmer* and *Broken Angels*. Her illustrations are on display at *www.artlair.com.*

Leia Weathington is a student at the Academy of Art in San Francisco and the creator of the popular Web comic series *Bold Riley*, which you can read online at both *www.girlamatic.com/comics/brww.php* and *www.webcomicsnation.com/redrabbit/.*

Well, here we are. Another volume of *Return to Labyrinth* in the can, thanks in no small part to the creativity and hard work of Messrs Jake T. Forbes and Chris Lie. I hope you enjoyed it. Are you still reeling from that ending as much as I was when I first read it?

The end of our second volume marks the halfway point of our story. Yes, you read that right. We're looking at four volumes here. Why the extra length? Well, that's partly on you. You see, after reading some of the responses to our first volume, it occurred to us that there are things fans want in a sequel to *Labyrinth* that we could give them if we had a little extra length. Besides, all of us were having far too much fun to stop at three volumes. So we decided to give ourselves an extra one. That said, don't think for a minute that you know where this story's going! I think we just might surprise you!

This is actually my first volume as editor of *Return to Labyrinth*, and I want to give a few shout-outs to some of the people who have contributed to the success of this series. First and foremost, we have our talented writer and artist, as well as all the amazing folks at The Jim Henson Company, especially James Formanek, Nicole Goldman and Halle Stanford. I also couldn't have gotten this book to the printer in time without the assistance of Sarah Tangney, and this series wouldn't exist at all without the efforts of Michael Polis and Rob Valois, both of whom have unfortunately moved on to other projects. And finally, we need to thank all of you—the *Labyrinth* fans—who have kept this universe alive in your hearts and minds for over twenty years now!

Thanks for reading! We'll see you in Volume 3!

Tim Beedle
Editor

P.S. Be sure to pick up our companion series *Legends of The Dark Crystal* when the first volume drops later this year. Because fans cannot live on *Labyrinth* alone!

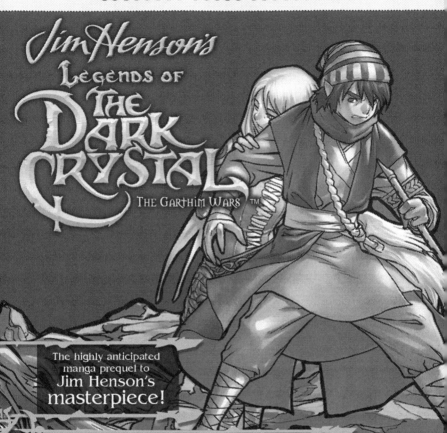

Jim Henson's
LEGENDS OF
THE DARK CRYSTAL
THE GARTHIM WARS ™

The highly anticipated manga prequel to **Jim Henson's masterpiece!**

THE DARK CRYSTAL BEGINS...

The original prequel to Jim Henson's fantasy epic is set centuries before *The Dark Crystal*, the groundbreaking film that won the hearts and minds of fans all over the world.

When the monstrous Garthim lay siege upon the Gelfling village of Namopo, it is up to Lahr, a Gelfling herder, to organize the resistance to save what is left of their land!

TM & © 1982, 2007 The Jim Henson Company. All Rights Reserved.
www.HENSON.com

FANTASY

T
TEEN
AGE 13+

FOR MORE INFORMATION VISIT: WWW.TOKYOPOP.COM

TOKYOPOP MANGA SUPPLEMENT

WHEN YOUR HEART IS DESPERATE
AND LONGS FOR SOMETHING LOST,
AN ALICHINO COULD PROVIDE IT,
BUT YOUR SOUL WILL PAY THE COST...

Alichino™

www.TOKYOPOP.com/alichino

©1998 Kouyu Shurei. ©2005 TOKYOPOP Inc.

TEEN
AGE 13+

www.TOKYOPOP.com